SIOBHAN COSTELLO

NETWORKING BITES

BITE 1

The Memorable Minute

Copyright Siobhan Costello

First published in 2015 by
Milton Contact Ltd

A CIP catalogue record for this book is available from
The British Library

ISBN: 978-0-9929289-6-4

All rights reserved. No part of this publication may be reproduced, stored in a retrieval system, or transmitted in any form or by any means – electronic, mechanical, photocopy, recording, or any other – except for brief quotations in print reviews, without prior permission of the author.

Cover design by DDS Media Group www.ddsmediagroup.co.uk
Author portrait by Helena g Anderson www.helena-g-anderson.com

Printed in United Kingdom

Milton Contact Ltd
3 Hall End, Milton, Cambridge, UK
CB24 6AQ

www.miltoncontact.co.uk

Dedication

To Steve

Acknowledgements

Kate Kelly, The Business Plumber
Kathryn Fletcher, Fletcher-Thompson Accountants
Cecilia Holden, Pink Web Solutions
Sally de Jong, Travel Counsellors
Rosalind Bubb, Rosalind Bubb EFT Practitioner
Mary Blackhurst Hill, Image Consultant

Introduction to Networking Bites

Welcome to the first in the series of Networking Bites – small bite-sized guides to help you build your business through face to face networking. Throughout this series I am going to give you top tips and ideas that will:

- ✓ Make you memorable long after you've left a network meeting
- ✓ Help you build your list of useful contacts
- ✓ Get referrals for your ideal clients
- ✓ Find referral partners and collaborators that will work with you to grow your business
- ✓ Get a return on your investment in networking.

This first bite, The Memorable Minute takes you through the process of writing a pitch that gets you the clients you really want to work with and a return on your networking investment.

Contents

Dedication	iii
Acknowledgements	iii
Introduction to Networking Bites	v
Contents	vii
The Memorable Minute	1
What is a Memorable Minute?	1
The Key Mistakes Business Owners Make	2
Why You Need to Get It Right	3
Your Memorable Minute Goal	5
Why You Need to Set a Goal	5
The Three Essential Parts of the Memorable Minute	6
Using Memorable Props Effectively	10
How to Deliver a Confident Pitch	11
Create a Library of Memorable Minutes	13
Conclusion	15
Sample Memorable Minutes	16
Contact Details	26
About the Author	27

Bite One
The Memorable Minute

In this Bite we will cover:

- What is a Memorable Minute?
- The key mistakes
- Why you need to get your Memorable Minute right!
- Your Memorable Minute Goal
- The three essential parts of the Memorable Minute
- How to use props effectively
- How to deliver a confident pitch

What is a Memorable Minute?

The Memorable Minute is often called the Elevator Pitch. It is based on the idea that if you found yourself in an elevator with your ideal client and had 60 seconds before it reached the ground floor, how would you pitch your business to them?

For your Memorable Minute to have an impact at a network meeting it needs to tell people who you are, what you do and what sort of business you are looking for.

It is the key element of many networking meetings and, done right, it can be a key strategy to help you build your business.

The Key Mistakes Business Owners Make

Firstly they don't write one! They arrive at a network meeting having never even thought about what they want to say about their business or the type of business they are looking for.

This results in them waffling about what they do and often happens to people who are new to networking. They give the history of how they have come into their business rather than stating clearly what they do. Because their message is not clear, the other networkers do not know what sort of clients or business contacts they are looking for. As a consequence they don't get any business.

Secondly, they are not specific. Use each meeting to advertise a different aspect of your business. You can't speak about everything you do in 60 seconds so sell one aspect really well.

Thirdly they don't ask for the type of business or clients they want. They focus on what business they think they will get from those in the room, rather than asking for a referral for their ideal client.

> **Top Tip!**
> **The more specific you are the better**

Why You Need to Get It Right

How many network meetings do you leave without anyone expressing an interest in what you do?

What about the money you spend on networking? Are you getting a return on your investment or do you feel it's a waste of your money because you're not getting any business?

Over time you begin to feel invisible and lose confidence, wondering if you will ever get any clients. You may even stop networking completely. Often those 60 seconds can stop people attending a network meeting because they see that one minute as terrifying. They don't prepare and lose vital opportunities to get business leads.

Simply put, when you get your Memorable Minute right, you will get business.

This is your sixty seconds to make an impact and to connect with your audience.

When you get it right you will stop wasting your valuable time and money and start getting a return on your investment.

Your confidence will grow because you will know you have a sustainable business and that people want to buy your services and products.

Your personal confidence will grow as you become more at ease with standing up and selling your business and your services.

You will only work with your ideal clients because other networkers will hear clearly who your target market is and will refer those clients to you.

Networking will do the work for you! When you get your Memorable Minute right, your networking colleagues will remember you and recommend you long after the meeting has finished.

You will attract referral partners who can see the link between their business and yours and can cross-refer to you. This is a great way to enhance your brand and build your business.

You may also attract collaborators which can give you an additional income stream through the development of a new service or product alongside your collaborator.

Figure 1. Why you need to get your Memorable Minute right

Your Memorable Minute Goal

Before you start networking, consider what your overall goal will be. Then, before each meeting, think about what type of referral will take you closer to achieving it.

Why You Need to Set a Goal

- ✓ Goals help you to focus on what you want
- ✓ They prevent you from getting distracted and give you direction
- ✓ If you know what you want you are more likely to achieve it.

Top Tip!

If you know what you want, you are more likely to achieve it

The Three Essential Parts of the Memorable Minute

You only have 60 seconds to make yourself memorable and while this may seem a huge task, it can be made very simple by breaking the Memorable Minute down into three discreet sections – the Opening, the Core and the Conclusion.

With that in mind let's look at each section in turn.

The Opening

This lasts 10 seconds only and is where you give the key details about your business.

Here you want to state:

- Your name
- The name of your company
- Your geographical area if appropriate.

Give one sentence summarising what you do. The purpose of this section is to focus your listeners' attention, so resist the urge to give a long list of your services and products at this point.

The Core

This is the body of the Memorable Minute and lasts 40 seconds only.

In this section give specific information about the one aspect of your business you want to promote at that event.

This is not a long shopping list of all of the things you do.

Focusing right from the start attracts your audience's attention.

Hook them with your first sentence. Start by saying 'This month I would like to tell you about…' Or ask a question. 'Who do you know who needs …?' Other networkers will take notice of what you say.

Be specific about the type of referral you are looking for. This ties back to your networking goal. Be effective and decide beforehand what it is you want from each networking meeting and then ask for it.

> **Top Tip!**
> **Hook them with your first sentence**

This section is all about holding the attention of those around the table. You might want to experiment with some of the following suggestions:

- Tell a story that shows how you work. People love stories and it is a great way to present what you do.
- Use case studies as examples to build a picture of the type of client or business you want to attract.
- Read out a testimonial from a client that demonstrates the effectiveness of your service.
- Tell them about the special promotion you are running that month.
- Sing a song or say a poem! See Mary Blackhurst Hill's Memorable Minute as an example of a great poem (See Sample Memorable Minutes later).
- Give them a call to action. Unless you tell people what you want them to do they won't do anything at all. It's just human nature. Tell them if you want them to email

you with a possible referral. Or do you want them to contact you by phone or do you want them to give their contact your business card?

- Avoid using any professional jargon. Some professions are filled with acronyms and words that only those in that profession will understand. Find another way to say it so that your message is clear to others.
- Use humour but only if it suits your personality and the nature of your business. Take a look at Sally de Jong's fun Memorable Minute in the Examples or Kathryn Fletcher's use of Valentine's Day to talk about her accountancy business.
- Give a top tip that might help other business owners. Inadvertently you are advertising your expertise, knowledge of your field and your services. This will build confidence in your brand and build relationships.
- Ask for business advice or a recommendation for a specific service you require. This is an excellent way to build relationships. And you will get contacts of recommended professionals already known to those on the group.

The Conclusion

This final part of your Memorable Minute is 10 seconds long. This is when you remind everyone who you are, your business name and if you've got a strapline say it now.

A strapline summarises what your business represents. If you don't have one, then it's worthwhile developing a strapline for your business as it sets you apart from your competition and helps people remember you. Think about

Figure 2. Examples of straplines

some famous straplines and you'll see how effective they are at being memorable.

You may think that this is repeating what you have already said before but even over the course of 60 seconds people may forget your name. So help them to remember you by repeating it at this point.

What should you do then? Sit down!

Remember you have 60 seconds and that's it. Resist the urge to go on and fill any available seconds you have left. If you do this your Minute will lose its impact and people will lose interest in you.

> **Top Tip!**
>
> For your Memorable Minute template go to: http://goo.gl/7TzG51

Using Memorable Props Effectively

Props make your business memorable. A prop is something that connects your business in the listeners' minds. It's a great way to be remembered in a room full of lots of people and separates you out from your competition.

If you make a product such as photographs, or you sell skincare products, then use these to demonstrate what you do in your Memorable Minute. A jeweller might hold up a particular piece of jewellery she wants to focus on that month.

If you don't have a product like this, then think creatively about a prop that might represent your business.

If you are a cake maker for example, then you might use a wooden spoon or a recipe book.

I've seen a Virtual Assistant who held up a china cup and saucer to show how she can release time for business owners to take a break.

Take a look at the photo of Kate Kelly, The Business Plumber in the examples at the back of the book to see her prop. She helps business owners to sort out their processes so that they can get paid faster and she uses a plunger to represent her business.

A will writer or a lawyer might bring a briefcase.

A representative from the charity Headway brings a plastic brain called Fred to show how the charity helped stroke victims.

Make your prop simple. You only have 60 seconds to make an impact. You don't want to use up your time getting organised or laying out your props around you.

> **Top Tip!**
>
> **Props: Keep it simple and be creative**

How to Deliver a Confident Pitch

Now you know what to put into your Memorable Minute you want to present it with confidence.

There are seven key ways to do this.

1. **Write and time your Memorable Minute**

    Before you go to a network meeting write your Memorable Minute. Time it and make sure your Memorable Minute is just that – one minute long.

2. **Practice, practice, practice**

    Stand in front of a mirror and say it until you feel you know the content very well.

3. **Stand up**

   Stand up when you deliver your Minute, even if others remain seated. By standing up you will project your voice effectively so that people will hear you.

4. **Speak slowly and clearly** so that you can be heard and understood.

5. **Make eye contact**

   This shows your openness and helps to build relationships and trust with everyone.

6. **If you can't remember** your Memorable Minute then read it out. Rosalind Bubb, EFT and TAT Practitioner, whose Memorable Minute is included in the Examples, always reads out her minute. This keeps her focused, on target and her message is always clear.

7. **Smile!**

   It's so simple, yet such an effective way to connect with other members.

As an added bonus Nina Cooke, Confidence Expert has recorded her top tips for presenting your Memorable Minute in which she gives her ten top tips for confident presentation.

Interview with Nina Cooke Confidence Coach

Create a Library of Memorable Minutes

If you use this approach to deliver your Memorable Minute you can replicate it time and time again to create a library of Minutes.

Using different annual events (e.g. Valentines' Day or Christmas), different types of clients, different products or services and case studies or testimonials, you can create Minutes for weekly and monthly network meetings throughout the year (Figure 3).

It is very important to evaluate the impact of each Memorable Minute you deliver. Keep a note of the ones that have had the most impact. And, if a pitch hasn't worked, make changes to make it more powerful.

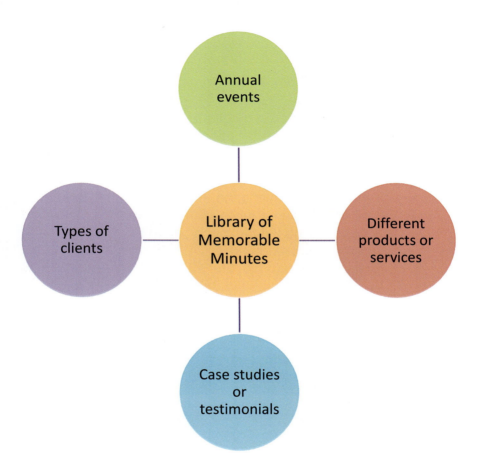

Figure 3. Library of Memorable Minutes

Conclusion

I hope you have enjoyed this short guide to writing your Memorable Minute. Being memorable in business isn't always easy but if you follow these simple steps you will start to see a return on your financial investment in networking.

Please visit my website www.greatbusinessresults.co.uk to find out how I can help you further with your networking strategy. Or visit my website www.thebestselleracademy.com if you would like help building a business from your book.

I wish you all the best in your business and look forward to connecting with you for future Networking Bites.

Best wishes,

Siobhan

Sample Memorable Minutes

Mary Blackhurst Hill

Image Consultant – working from the inside out.

It's January – time for resolution
Time to find that dieting solution
But before you shrink
I'd like you to think
About joining me in revolution
We women come in variety packs
Some size minimum, some size max
The media claim
We should all be the same
Let's not listen to those journalist hacks
Think of the words that describe the real you
The woman who's soul is utterly true
Are you luscious and curvy
Or neurotic and nervy?
Is it cake or your nails that you chew?
Now some girls stay effortlessly slim
Some struggle to stay reasonably trim
But we can all look great
Whatever our weight
Without selling our soul to the gym
Because variety is a joy forever
Size ten for all – no, never
We'll dress our shape not our size
Despise Media Lies
Self-acceptance and love makes us clever
So if you are voluptuous, scrumptious, bountiful, forceful, powerful, irresistible, cuddly, sexy, all woman?
Celebrate it! You don't need a diet, you need an image consultation.

helping you to be happy, effective and well

Hello, my name is Rosalind and I am a therapist.

I help people to be happy, effective and well *[demonstrate technique]* using EFT, Emotional Freedom Techniques, sometimes known as "tapping."

It's like emotional acupuncture, but without the needles.

This month I'm wondering, who do you know who has experienced an unpleasant event, or a trauma?

It could be a car crash, an accident, a fire; or some kind of violence or attack; or some kind of medical trauma.

Who do you know who hasn't been themselves, since this happened?

Who is struggling with the impact of it? Wants to get back to normal, but has no idea how to do that?

It can be much easier than you might think.

I can help people to recover, to put it behind them, to feel peaceful and well and in control once more. I make the process easy and painless – and safe.

I can work with people face-to-face, on the telephone, and on Skype, so it doesn't matter where they're based.

That's Rosalind Bubb, "tapping" and TAT – helping you to be happy, effective and well.

travel counsellors

Sally de Jong
Travel Counsellor

Welcome on board Travel Counsellors flight number QUOTE 123 to your dream holiday. Our aircraft today is under the command of Captain Sally de Jong. Our flying time will be approximately one minute.

In preparation for take-off please ensure that I know your preferences and budget, your names match your passports, and that your internet browser is turned off. Federal Aviation Regulations require you to comply with following the advice of your Travel Counsellor and to benefit from their experience! The NO SHOPPING AROUND ON THE INTERNET sign will remain illuminated for the duration of the flight, and calls to other travel agents are prohibited throughout the cabin and in the lavatories. All lavatories are equipped with shopping around detection systems and Federal Law prohibits tampering with, disabling, or destroying these systems.

While we are here to ensure that you have a comfortable flight with us, we are also concerned about your safety. With that in mind, please read the Travel Counsellors financial protection leaflet in the seat pocket in front of you.

There are eight emergency exits on this aircraft. In the unlikely event of an emergency your Travel Counsellor will provide full assistance.

On behalf of the entire Travel Counsellors crew, thank you for flying with Travel Counsellors. We realise that you do have a choice of travel agent, but we look forward to having you on board again soon.

When booking your holiday don't get it wrong, book with your Travel Counsellor Sally de Jong.

Business Plumber

Kate Kelly
The Business Plumber

Good afternoon – my name is Kate Kelly, the Business Plumber.

I help businesses work smarter rather than working harder.

Sometimes that means doing different things, sometimes doing them in a different way.

And sometimes it means stop doing things altogether!

One of my favourite examples is quoted by Robert Sobel, an American professor of history –

"In 1803 the British Civil Service posted a man to stand on the Cliffs of Dover with a telescope.

He was instructed to ring a bell if he saw Napoleon and his army coming across the English Channel.

That position was finally abolished . . . in 1945 – 124 years after the death of Napoleon!"

If that's ringing any bells for a business you know – give them my card!

The Business Plumber – helping your work flow – and your profits grow!

SEARCHING GOOGLE FOR IMAGES

I'm Cecilia Holden from Pink Web Solutions. We offer fixed price affordable web design and search engine optimisation to local businesses.

Did you know that the same copyright rules that apply to text also apply to images? We often tend to forget because they're just pictures, but you should not just pick images you fancy from other websites or from Google images and add them to your own website or marketing material.

You can now search Google for images, finding all pages matching your picture rather than your keyword. Suppose you decide you want to rebrand, and you have a beautiful shiny new logo. You may want to see if anyone else has anything similar, or if your old logo still exists on the internet. You can also use this method to check whether any of your images are being used without your permission, or how many other companies are using a particular stock image that you are planning to use in your marketing. The possibilities are endless.

Start by opening Google. Do this by going to www.google.com or www.google.co.uk rather than just using a Google search bar. You will know you're in the right place because you'll see the big Google logo in the middle of the screen. In the top right corner, you will see a little checkerboard of tools, or maybe a list of tools. Click on Images.

Now click back in the search bar in the centre of the screen and you will notice that a camera icon has appeared. If you click that, Google will then invite you to upload or paste the URL of an image. Do this and then press search. Google will now be searching for matches for your image.

Pink Web Solutions – taking the phobe out of technophobe

Good afternoon. My name is Kathryn Fletcher and I run Fletcher Thompson Chartered Accountants, based in Suffolk.

So how was your Valentine's Day?

Did you go to see the latest over hyped film based on another book franchise?

Did you go out to a restaurant and pay for an overpriced meal and sit there in silence with all the other couples that don't talk to each every other day of the year?

Did you keep it simple and curl up on the sofa with your loved one watching a lovely romcom, only for him to turnover halfway through because the rugby or football highlights were on?

Or maybe you were catching up with your accounts as the tax year end is looming and you want to get your accounts done quickly this year.

If the answer was one of the first three then I am sure there is someone else in the room today that can help you. If however if was the last one and you would prefer to do something a little more romantic on Valentines or any other Saturday night, then please get in touch so we can help you out with your bookkeeping

Kathryn Fletcher, Fletcher Thompson Chartered Accountants. Helping you regain the romance in your life.

Imagine you were asked to speak on a stage in front of your target audience.

What would be your reaction?

Would you think:

"What a fantastic opportunity, I can't wait to get out there and tell them how I can help them."

Or would you think:

"I'd rather die than do that!"

If it's the latter reaction, it's just your thoughts telling you, "Who am I to do that? Who is going to listen to me? I'm not important enough. It's safer to stay invisible."

These thoughts are your limiting beliefs, stopping you from stepping up and shining in your business, and being even more successful.

If you or anyone you know would like to know how to be unstoppable and have the confidence and courage to say "Yes" to wonderful opportunities and greater business success, just get in touch. I'd love to know how I can help you.

My name is Nina Cooke at www.ninacooke.co.uk.

Contact Details

Siobhan Costello, Great Business Results
Email: info@greatbusinessresults.co.uk
Website: www.greatbusinessresults.co.uk

The Bestseller Academy
Email: info@thebestselleracademy.com
Website: www.thebestselleracademy.com

Sally de Jong, Travel Counsellor
Email: sally.dejong@travelcounsellors.com
Website: www.travelcounsellors.co.uk/sally.dejong

Mary Blackhurst Hill
Email: mary.blackhurst.hill@houseofcolour.co.uk
Website: www.houseofcolour.co.uk/maryblackhursthill

Rosalind Bubb, EFT and TAT Practitioner
Email: rosalind@eft-tapping.co.uk
Website: www.rosalindb.com

Kate Kelly, The Business Plumber
Email: kate@businessplumber.co.uk
Website: www.businessplumber.co.uk

Cecilia Holden, Pink Web Solutions
Email: cecilia@pinkwebsolutions.co.uk
Website: www.pinkwebsolutions.co.uk

Kathryn Fletcher, Fletcher Thompson Accountants
Email: kathryn@fletcher-thompson.co.uk
Website: www.fletcher-thompson.co.uk

About the Author

Siobhan Costello is founder of Great Business Results and The Bestseller Academy and runs seven successful network groups for business women in the UK.

She is passionate about showing other women how they can build their businesses.

"Remaining true to yourself is the best way to promote your business and get a return on your networking investment."

Previously, Siobhan had a long nursing career and also ran a successful business as a hypnotherapist and Master NLP Practitioner.

At first she hated networking, the pushy way some people could be at a meeting and the way she felt she had to 'perform'. It just didn't feel right!

Then she discovered that there are key ways to make networking enjoyable. More importantly, she began to see her business grow through getting out there and networking in a way that felt authentic to her.

The Memorable Minute is the first in a series of Networking Bites that complement Siobhan's 5 Step Programme for Confident Networking.

"The Memorable Minute helps you deliver your message with impact, so that you can get quality referrals and leads and build your business as a result."